New Zealand

The Ultimate New Zealand Travel Guide By A Traveler For A Traveler
The Best Travel Tips: Where To Go, What To See And Much More.

SECOND EDITION

Table of Contents

intensified over time due to the continuous encroachment by British settlers.

Chapter 2: The Basics

A. Time Zones
The local time zone is 12 hours past the GMT so you should adjust your timepiece accordingly.

B. Climate and Weather
The local weather can be volatile so you should prepare beforehand. Note that New Zealand is a two-season country with average temperatures for winter and summer falling between 10-15 and 20-30 °C respectively.

C. Currency
The main unit of currency is the New Zealand dollar (NZ$) but most establishments accept all major credit cards. Although there is no limit as to how much can be brought in or taken out, a Border Cash Report will be required from those who are in possession of NZ$10,000 or more in cash. Currency can be exchanged at most hotels, local banks, and Bureau de Change kiosks around the city.

D. Visas and Immigration
Disembarkation practices in the country are quite standard so you can expect the usual documents checking, customs declarations, and luggage screening to take place. A detailed list of what cannot be brought into the country can be found at the New Zealand Customs Service website (www.customs.govt.nz).

There are no restrictions on foreigners entering the country but a valid passport or visa (if required from their home country) plus other pertinent travel documents will be required. More information can be found at Immigration New Zealand (www.immigration.govt.nz)

Why Lost Travelers Guides?

First, we want to wish you an amazing time in New Zealand when you plan to visit. Also we would like to thank you and congratulate you for downloading our travel guide, *"New Zealand; The Ultimate New Zealand Travel Guide By A Traveler For A Traveler"*.

Allow us to explain our beginnings, and the reason we created Lost Travelers. Lost Travelers was created due to one simple problem that other guides on the market did not solve; loss of time. Considering it's the 21st century and everything is available online, why do we still purchase guidebooks? To save us time! That's right.

Since the goal is to be efficient and save time, we did not understand why there are several guidebooks on the market that are of 500 to 1000 page' long. We do not believe one needs that much bluff to get an overview of the location and some remarkable suggestions. Considering many guidebooks on the market are filled with "suggestions" that were sponsored for, we have decided to take a different approach and provide our travelers with an honest opinion and decline any sort of sponsorship. This simply allows us to cut off any nonsense and create our guides the Lost Travelers style.

Our mission is simple; to create an easy to follow guide book that outlines the best of activities to do in our limited time at the destination. This easily saves you your most valuable asset; your time. You no longer need to spend hours looking through a massive book, or spend hours searching for information on the internet as we have completed the whole process for you. The best part is we provide you our e-guides for one third the price of the leading brand, and our paper copy for only half the price.

Thanks again for choosing us, we hope you enjoy!

Chapter 1: Culture and History

Located 2,012 km to the south of Australia is New Zealand. There are two main islands comprising it, the North and South islands, and outlying islands scattered within the vicinity. Its two main islands are separated by a body of water known as the Cook Strait. The North Island is 829 km long. Its southern end is volcanic and because of this, there are plenty of excellent hot springs and geysers in the area. On the South island, lie the Southern Alps by the west end. Here is where one will find the highest point in New Zealand that is Mount Cook. It is 12,316 feet tall!

Some of the outlying islands are inhabited while others are not. The inhabited islands include Chatham, Great Barrier, and Stewart islands. The largest of the uninhabited islands are Campbell, Kermadec, Antipodes, and Auckland islands.

The first inhabitants of New Zealand were the Maoris. Their initial population was only 1,000 people. According to their oral history, it took the initial Maori population seven canoes to reach New Zealand from other parts of Polynesia. It was in the mid-1600s that the island cluster was explored by a man named Abel Tasma, a Dutch navigator. Another foreigner, a British by the name of James Cook, engaged in three voyages to New Zealand the first one taking place in 1769. New Zealand became a formal annex to Britain during the mid 1800s.

During this time, the Treaty of Waitangi was signed between Britain and the Maoris. It stated that there would be ample protection for Maori land should the Maoris accept British rule. Despite the treaty, tension between both factions

I. Facilities for the Disabled
Local regulations demand that buildings have ample access facilities for people with disabilities.

Accommodation for the Disabled
Although access provisions are readily available, smaller establishments like hostels and inns may not have other mobility provisions for the disabled. This is because of their limited area. Larger commercial accommodation providers do have rooms that offer these services. The same goes for commercial establishments around New Zealand. More information about disabled access can be found at www.accomobility.co.nz.

Transport for the Disabled
Public transport provisions offer access and special provisions for the disabled. For tour operators, be sure to notify them in advance so that they can accommodate any necessity whatsoever.

Parking Access
Parking lots offer spaces especially marked for the disabled. Concessions like display cards and disability-parking permits must be available before these spaces can be occupied. A home mobility card or a medical certificate can be presented for these to be issued. Apply for the necessary permits through the CCS Disability Action (0800 227 225). More information can be found at www.ccsdisabilityaction.org.nz.

J. Recommended City Apps
Apps are very useful when traveling to New Zealand. They offer information on the best places to visit, sights too see, food to eat, events to attend, and promotions visitors can enjoy during their vacation. Here are some of the best apps to have:

E. Electricity and Communication
The local electricity supply runs at 230/240 volts and angled two or three-pin plugs are used. Most hotels provide AC sockets at 110 volts (20 watts).

F. Internet and Wi-Fi Access
There are establishments and areas that offer free Wi-Fi access. You can also purchase a temporary Internet connection plan from one of New Zealand's local networks (average cost is NZ$19):

- Vodafone
- 2degrees
- Spark
- Skinny

G. Booking a Trip
Summer is New Zealand's peak season running from November to March followed by winter during April to October.

H. Visitor Information Centers
You can find local information, advice, and trip suggestions when they visit one of the eighty i-SITE Visitor Information Centers around New Zealand. This is the country's official visitor information network. Popular destinations, transport services, accommodations providers, local businesses and retailers, restaurants, activities, current events, and other related news and updates can be found on their Be Accessible website. Free maps, weather, and mountain safety information can also be found here.

Chapter 2: The Basics

A. Time Zones
The local time zone is 12 hours past the GMT so you should adjust your timepiece accordingly.

B. Climate and Weather
The local weather can be volatile so you should prepare beforehand. Note that New Zealand is a two-season country with average temperatures for winter and summer falling between 10-15 and 20-30 °C respectively.

C. Currency
The main unit of currency is the New Zealand dollar (NZ$) but most establishments accept all major credit cards. Although there is no limit as to how much can be brought in or taken out, a Border Cash Report will be required from those who are in possession of NZ$10,000 or more in cash. Currency can be exchanged at most hotels, local banks, and Bureau de Change kiosks around the city.

D. Visas and Immigration
Disembarkation practices in the country are quite standard so you can expect the usual documents checking, customs declarations, and luggage screening to take place. A detailed list of what cannot be brought into the country can be found at the New Zealand Customs Service website (www.customs.govt.nz).

There are no restrictions on foreigners entering the country but a valid passport or visa (if required from their home country) plus other pertinent travel documents will be required. More information can be found at Immigration New Zealand (www.immigration.govt.nz)

intensified over time due to the continuous encroachment by British settlers.

Apps List

- Walk Auckland
- Where to Next
- Neat Places
- Welly Walks
- Pure New Zealand
- Zomato
- MetService
- Google Maps
- CamperMate
- StarChart

K. Qualmark Seal

New Zealand has quality standards applied to local businesses. Establishments are independently assessed against these standards and receive a Qualmark seal if they satisfy the general requirements. The seal can be used to identify professional and trustworthy businesses across the country.

L. Health and Safety

The country is recognized as one of the healthiest in the world both for locals and travelers alike. Unlike its neighboring countries, diseases such as typhoid and malaria have never manifested, making it an excellent destination for children and adults. When it comes to the local wildlife, the species found here are not classified as dangerous.

Vaccinations

There are no vaccination requirements for those who wish to visit New Zealand however individuals may choose to abide by

WHO-suggested vaccines for hepatitis B, polio, rubella, chickenpox, measles, mumps, diphtheria, and tetanus; all standard vaccinations. In this case, it would be best to carry an International Certificate of Vaccination. This yellow booklet can be obtained from one's attending physician.

Infectious Diseases
There is one type of infectious disease that is rampant in the area so be sure to take caution. Giardiasis results from the giardia parasite, which is widespread in New Zealand waterways. Do avoid consuming any untreated water from streams and lakes.

Health Insurance and Hospitals
Adequate health insurance is necessary. It should provide comprehensive coverage at a reasonable rate. See to it that overseas medical expenses are included in the policy and make a list of the requirements needed to make the necessary reimbursements back home.

New Zealand provides access to various hospital establishments, both public and private, where a high standard of care can be expected. Public hospitals offer free services to residents while travelers will be required to present their insurance policies.

If care is necessary due to an accident that occurred in the country, the traveler will get the needed medical assistance free of charge. It will be covered by the ACC (Accident Compensation Corporation).

Emergency Medical Assistance
For emergency health advice, you can contact New Zealand's Health line - a 24-hour free-call service (0800 611 116).

Pharmaceuticals
Medications are readily accessible but dispensaries will require the original labeled containers and prescriptions. Any signs of tampering will deem these invalid.

M. Getting Around

Traveling to New Zealand by Air
There are several airports in the country with Auckland serving as the busiest one of all:
Auckland International Airport

- Christchurch International Airport

- Dunedin International Airport

- Hamilton International Airport

- Queenstown Airport

- Rotorua International Airport

- Wellington Airport

Palmerston North Airport
The local international carrier is Air New Zealand but there are many commercial and chartered flights that come and go from various points across the globe. Unless travelers come in from Australia, a flight to and from New Zealand can cost a lot of money and this is why advanced bookings are suggested.

The airports are busy the entire year because various events are scattered among the twelve months. The busiest time of year for the country is over the Christmas period, mid-summer, and during the skiing season.

Depending on which airport travelers will be flying from, departure taxes will be charged as follows: A separate charge of NZ$25 for adults and NZ$10 for children 12 and under in Hamilton, Rotorua, and Palmerston North. The fee for airports in Auckland, Christchurch, Dunedin, Queenstown, and Wellington, NZ$12.50 is already included in the ticket price.

Traveling to New Zealand by Sea
Travelers hailing from nearby Australia or other Pacific islands can choose to head on off to New Zealand by sea. A number of passenger cruise liners pass through New Zealand so it will be a good idea to check these out. An alternative would be to consider a berth on a freighter or cargo ship. Excellent companies to contact include P&O Cruises (www.pocruises.com.au), Freighter Expeditions (www.freighterexpeditions.com.au), and Freighter Cruises (www.freightercruises.com).

Chapter 3: Auckland

Aside from being the most populated city in New Zealand, Auckland is also the largest one in the country but it does not serve as its capital. It is a tourist city that offers a number of different urban attractions. There is also a wide array of food choices that visitors can try out. Every age group can find some activity suitable for them here.

Accommodations

The average price for a bed in a hostel dorm is NZ$15-40 while private provisions cost about NZ$60-90. Those who are interested in budget hotels can find accommodations priced at NZ$65-100 a night. It is quite expensive to stay here because it is a city center but a short distance out of Auckland, travelers can find rooms that cost about only NZ$40.

Here are some of the best-rated accommodations in Auckland:

HILTON AUCKLAND

The Hilton in Auckland is your premier destination for all things classy. The rooms here are equipped with all the best amenities. The rooms are extremely spacious and have balconies that overlook breath-taking views. The seafood served here is quite delectable and the restaurant provides an amazing view. The external amenities include heated pools and exercise rooms that are complimentary.

Princes Wharf, 147 Quay Street
00 64 9 978 2000

QUAY WEST SUITES AUCKLAND

Located just 7 minutes from the sky tower, this city hotel is a great place for you to stay in Auckland. The place is an apartment hotel that provides 1 and 2 bedroom apartments. The room service facility provided here is quite good and will make for a comfortable stay. There are many amenities on offer here including the heated pool, a sauna and a restaurant.

8 Albert Street
00 64 9 309 6000

MOLLIES

This is a boutique hotel that provides some great amenities to its guests. The suites are extremely comfortable and come with features such as Wi-Fi, television, minibars etc. you will also have access to kitchenettes where you can cook for yourself. The place also offers a whirlpool bath that you can enjoy with your friends and family.

6 Tweed Street, St Mary's Bay
00 64 9 376 3489

Other options
- COTTER HOUSE
4 St Vincent Avenue, Remuera
00 64 9 529 5156

- RYDGES HARBOURVIEW
Corner of Federal & Kingston Streets
00 64 9 3755900

- STAMFORD PLAZA AUCKLAND
22 Lower Albert Street
00 64 9 309 8888

- SHAKESPEARE BREWERY & HOTEL
61 Albert Street (at Corner of Wyndam & Albert Streets)
00 64 9 373 5396

- THE HERITAGE AUCKLAND
22-24 Nelson Street
00 64 9 379 8553

- THE PEACE & PLENTY INN
6 Flagstaff Terrace, Devonport
00 64 9 445 2925

- WESTIN LIGHTER QUAY
21 Viaduct Harbour Avenue
00 64 9 909 9000

Food and Beverage

A number of commercial dining establishments can be found here where budget meals can be bought at about NZ$7-23. For fancier restaurants, the average cost is NZ$30 per plate while home cooking will require a decent budget of NZ$60-75.

Auckland has a wide selection of restaurants guaranteed to satisfy even the fussiest of eaters.

Restaurants in Auckland

Auckland plays host to top class restaurants, each of which is unique in its own way. You can find food restaurants under your budget with ease thanks to Auckland's size.

Dine by Peter Gordon

Celebrity chef Peter Gordon's restaurant tops the list of must visit hotels in Auckland. Located on the 3rd floor of the Skycity hotel, the place serves out a delicious a la carte menu that is sure to satisfy your senses. The Cambridge duck breast here is the most recommended dish on the menu. The miso salmon is not far behind and is sure to please your palate.

90 Federal Street, Auckland, 00 64 9 363 7030; www.skycityauckland.co.nz

Euro

For all those looking to pamper themselves with some fresh organic food can visit the Euro. The place is famous for serving out some of the best homegrown foods and offers a delectable menu. You might have to reserve a table in advance though as the crowd here builds up pretty fast. To put it in their own words, "Simple and elegant, traditional but flavorsome, easy on the eye and palate" is the restaurant's USP.

Shed 22, Princes Wharf, Auckland, 00 64 9 309 9866; www.eurobar.co.nz

Sails

Sails is a restaurant in Westhaven Marina that is famous for its location and brilliant atmosphere. The food served here is simply superb and will leave you wanting more. The beef with horseradish and mushroom is the most recommended dish on the menu and so is the amazing seafood. The place is open for lunch from Monday through Friday with dinner being served every night of the week.

Westhaven Marina, Westhaven Drive, Auckland, 00 64 9 378 9890; www.sailsrestaurant.co.nz

Nightclubs/bars in Auckland

Twenty-one
Located in Skycity, Twenty-one is one of Auckland's best nightclubs. Right from its world class DJ to lip smacking cocktails; you are sure to have a great time here. The interiors here are uber chic and sure to mesmerize you. Wednesdays here are industry night with Fridays and Saturdays being DJ nights. Once you step into this club, rest assured, you are not going to leave here before the wee hours of the morning.

SKYCITY, 72 Victoria Street West, Auckland, +64 9 363 6000

Bungalow 8
Bungalow 8 is a top class nightclub in Auckland that has played host to the world's who's who. The place offers some amazing drinks with the setting here being uber classy. Bungalow 8 is sure to leave you mesmerized and let you have a great time. The place boasts of having hosted celebrities the likes of who includes Richard Branson and Justin Timberlake.

48 Market Place, Auckland CBD, Auckland, 09 307 1500

Globe bar
If you are looking for a traveler pub then globe bar is your best choice. The place is usually bustling with travelers and expats all looking to find a new people. The globe bar is known for its wild parties that it holds almost every night of the week. The

place is world famous for hosting some of the best parties. You can kick back, relax and get yourself a drink or dance the night away.

Darby Street, Auckland CBD, Auckland, Call 09) 357 3980

Transportation

A local bus service can be accessed throughout the day with fare costing NZ$2.50 for short distances up to NZ$10.50 for trips around the city. Along Queen Street runs the link bus. This service runs in ten-minute intervals. Each trip costs about NZ$2.

There is also a train system with an average fare of NZ$2. You could save a lot of money if you opted for the AT HOP. It is a hop on hop off service with an unlimited-use daily rate of NZ$16. When traveling to Rangitoto and Waiheke, do ride the ferry. Expect a round trip ticket to set you back about NZ$36.

What to Do

ENJOY A GAME OF CRICKET
Avid fans of cricket can watch games for free. During the weekends, local teams play exhibition games at Victoria Park. You can also join in if you think you are good enough.

VISIT AUCKLAND DOMAIN
This is a large park in the middle of the city. When the weather permits, a number of locals visit the park to jog, play sports, and hang around. Several walking trails can be found here and it is also an excellent place to visit for those who love to be surrounded by beautiful gardens.

OTARA FLEA MARKET

Saturdays are when the Otara flea market operates. It is a Maori and Polynesian market where visitors can find different offerings of clothes, local items, and foodstuffs. With a little engagement comes a ton of amazing deals not to mention fanciful and mouthwatering fare.

HAURAKI GULF

The gulf is known to have a wide variety of amazing sea life. It also offers different activities like boating and sailing not to mention scuba diving, whale watching, and good old fishing.

AUCKLAND ZOO

The local zoo is home to over 150 different animal species. There are over 500 animals here so the zoo established a series of habitat enclosures to ensure that the animals have a suitable place to reside in. Its pride lands and rainforest attractions are some of the most popular ones amongst visitors.

MOTAT

The Museum of Transport and Technology is an interactive museum that showcases about 300,000 items related to the fields of technology and transportation. The entrance fee is NZ$16. It is located close to the local zoo.

BUNGEE JUMPING

The man who created the sport operates a bungee jumping facility in the area. The jumps organized by AJ Hackett starts atop a bridge where jumpers leap into the harbor below.

SKY TOWER

Another amazing location for those without a fear of heights is the Sky Tower. It is the tallest tower in the southern part of the world rising 1000 feet into the sky. It offers panoramic views of Auckland, access to a revolving restaurant, and access to the city casino.

AQUARIUM
The local sea life aquarium offers travelers a glimpse into a wide array of fish, most of which can be found in the local area. There are impressive displays of stingrays and sharks suspended atop a transparent tunnel. The facility also has a winter exhibit.

MURIWAI GANNET COLONY
Breeding gannet birds can be found all through the stretch of the Muriwai beach. These birds nest between the sand dunes and can be found in the area come August until March. There are designated viewing platforms where visitors can watch the birds from a safe distance. Aside from bird watching, Muriwai is also an excellent destination for activities such as biking, hiking, and surfing.

HISTORICAL VILLAGE AT HOWICK
You will be transported back in time when you pay the Howick Village a visit. It is considered to be one of the world's finest living museums where staff members dress in period costumes and speak in a manner reflective of the 1800s.

WAIKUMETE CEMETERY
Waikumete is the largest cemetery in the world and is home to the Corban family museum not to mention several other heritage infrastructures. Despite the eeriness, it is actually a fun experience to walk around the cemetery. There are free tours offered every first Sunday of the month where you will see tombstones as old as time itself.

WAITAKERE RANGES

Be treated to the sight of impressive waterfalls at the Waitakere Ranges. The area is quite rocky but offers access to a handful of beautiful beaches. It would be best to take a day trip here.

NORTH SHORE

The North Shore is the main beach in Auckland. It is frequented not only by tourists but locals as well. This is the place to visit for an active nightlife experience. Aside from this, it is also a hotspot for surfers. It surely is one of the must-visit locations in the city.

Chapter 4: Franz Josef

You will find a city by the name of Franz Josef here. It was named after a glacier, the Franz Josef Glacier, which was first explored back in 1865. This glacier is located about three miles from the main town and it only takes about twenty minutes of walking to reach its terminal face.

Aside from this particular glacier, Franz Josef is also known for being an excellent jumping point if you want to see other glaciers in the area, as there is more than one of them in town. The city is located in the South Island where ice tunnels also come aplenty.

Accommodations
An average hostel bed would cost around NZ$20-25 a night but a private room would cost NZ$55-90 on average. Hotels start at around NZ$50 a night per room.

Here are some of the best-rated accommodations in Franz Josef:

TE WAONUI FOREST RETREAT
Enshrouded by rainforest, this place is a gem of a place. The rooms are quite airy and modern and make for the perfect setting for a romantic escapade. There are basic features available in the room including television, Wi-Fi and minibar. You can have clear views of the forests from here, making for an amazing stay. You can also take advantage of the spa treatments available here.

3 Wallace Street, Off State Highway 6, Westland National Park

ASPEN COURT MOTEL FRANZ JOSEF

The rooms in this hotel are extremely spacious and well maintained. You can easily access the city center from here and enjoy your shopping. The rooms come with standard amenities such as television, minibar and also a kitchenette that you can use to prepare your meals. The views provided by the hotel are quite amazing and will allow you to take in the beauty of Franz Josef.

76 Cron Street, Westland National Park
00 64 6 880 309

ALPINE GLACIER MOTOR LODGE

The alpine glacier motor lodge is located in a suburban area against the backdrop of some amazing mountains. The rooms here are provided with all the requisite amenities that will help you avail a pleasant stay. You can access the many features that are provided by the lodge such as the room service and the whirlpool bath, which a big feature at this hotel.

17 Cron Street, Westland National Park

Other options

- 10 COTTAGES

8 Graham Place, Westland National Park

- THE TERRACE MOTEL

15 Cowan Street, Box 44, Westland National Park

- PUNGA GROVE MOTEL & SUITES

40 Cron Street, Westland National Park
00 64 4 488 7251

- **GLACIER VIEW MOTEL**
State Highway 6, Westland National Park

- **58 ON CRON MOTEL**
58 Cron Street, Westland National Park
00 64 9 887 8427

- **FRANZ JOSEF OASIS**
State Highway 6, Franz Josef North, Westland National Park

- **SCENIC HOTEL FRANZ JOSEF GLACIER HOTEL**
State Highway 6, P.O. Box 47, Westland National Park

Food and Beverage

NZ$22 is the average cost per meal in a restaurant here while self-cooking will cost about NZ$60-100 per week. Fast food options are also readily available and it will set you back around NZ$8 a meal.

Restaurants in Franz Josef

Most of the restaurants in Franz Josef are small but serve some amazing food. The ambience of most of the restaurant is homely and comforting.

The Landing

The Landing is hands down the best place to visit in Franz Josef to grab a quick bite. The place will always have something or the other going on like a quiz, a game or just a party. The food here is delectable and will help you regain your energy after a long trek. It's a happy place that does not fuss over décor and serves the purpose of a good restaurant.

State Highway 6, Franz Josef Glacier 7886, New Zealand, P:+64 3-752 0229

Canvas restaurant

The canvas restaurant is an amazing little place with some of the best views. The place offers some authentic meals that are quite tasty. There is also a bar attached to the place where you can savor some amazing drinks. The whitebaits and lamb shanks here are the most recommended on the menu.

State Highway 6, Franz Josef Glacier, New Zealand P: +64 3 752 0729

Wild cafe

The wild café located in Kiwi center is a great place to grab a quick bite. Located inside the wildlife center, the place is always full of people looking to grab a coffee and a sandwich. There are also many choices such as cakes and cookies that are simply delicious. Once you are done, you can pay a visit to the Kiwis and have a fun photo session.

Cowan St, Franz Josef Glacier 7886, New Zealand, P:+64 3-752 0600

Glacier base café

The glacier base café is busy visitor café that you can visit for a good snack. The place also offers light meals that are sure to satisfy your palate. You must make it a point to try the teas here that are known for their awesome taste. Once you are done eating, you can visit the hot pools located next door.

69 Cron St, Franz Josef Glacier 7886, New Zealand

Nightclubs/bars in Franz Josef

Snakebite brewery
Snakebite brewery is a great little place for you to try out in Franz Josef. The place is like a regular pub and serves some amazing brews. You can have a good time here with friends and family. The brewery is also known to serve some delectable meals that are sure to make your tummy very happy. The place is child friendly where children can savor great food.

28 Main Rd, Franz Josef Glacier 7886, New Zealand, +64 3-752 0234

Monsoon bar
Located on west coast, the monsoon bar is a great little place to grab a drink with your friends. The cozy little place offers you some amazing drinks, cocktails and other delicious brews. The food here is also recommended and will go well with your drink. You will have an amazing time digging into a hot meal while the weather outside pours down.

46 Cron St, Franz Josef Glacier 7886, New Zealand, +64 3-752 0220

Transportation
The thing about Franz Josef is that it is a rather small town that you can walk around easily, but there is also ample transportation for those who want to pay the glaciers a visit. There are tour coaches, cars, and buses that service the glacier tours. These can also bring you to and from town.

What to Do

GLACIER TOUR
A glacier tour would only take about half a day and is an excellent option for those who are working with a limited budget. Those who have time and money to spare can engage in longer glacier tours. There is more than one glacier that can be visited in this part of New Zealand.

HIKING TRAILS
The area offers amazing hiking trails that are more affordable. Walking through these trails offers an excellent view of the Franz Josef scenery.

HELICOPTER RIDE
Another excellent way to see the sights is via helicopter. Chartered rides are available daily but may come at a significant expense.

HUKAWAI GLACIER CENTER
This particular facility offers a one-of-a-kind glacier experience. It also offers an educational display about the country's glaciers, wildlife, geology, and Maori culture. A great activity to engage in inside the center is ice wall climbing.

HELI-HIKING ADVENTURE
Heli-hiking is a unique activity that can be experienced by Franz Josef visitors. A helicopter will take you over the glaciers then they can try their skills at hiking on the ice. The great thing about heli-hiking is that the helicopter gives you the opportunity to reach and hike over more remote areas.

GLACIER TREKKING

A full-day glacier hike experience includes trekking down the icy tunnels. This is an activity that should not be missed when a trip to Franz Josef is planned.

RIVER RAFTING

There are river-rafting tours across the Perth and Whataroa rivers in Franz Josef. These rivers can be found on the northern part of the city and are best visited during the summer months. They are excellent locations for whitewater rafting, as rapids of varying degrees are naturally available.

GLACIER HOT POOLS

There is a series of outdoor thermal baths in this part of the country that offer an excellent soak for those who want some much needed rest and relaxation. Massage services are also available here and offers a perfect escape after a day of hiking and glacier trekking.

HORSEBACK RIDING

You should also engage in horseback riding here. There is a trail ride that will bring you across the lush forests of Franz Josef. A typical trip runs for about six hours and it crosses remote beaches and farm lands as well.

RAINFOREST TREKKING

Trekking trails across the local rainforest are available to those who simply love to explore. All that is needed is a pack, water, snacks, and of course, a reliable pair of hiking shoes. Be careful, as the trails can be muddy and slippery.

MOUNTAIN BIKE

Trails can also be accessed and explored via mountain bike. In Franz Josef, there are rental service providers offering bikes for a fee of NZ$25 for a half day of use.

SKYDIVING

Here is where adrenalin junkies can jump off of a plane at a height of 18000 feet. There are limited locations that offer this height for skydiving. A typical charge for this activity is NZ$300 per person which gets them a different view of all the mountains, rivers, rainforests, and glaciers in the area.

WEST COAST WILDLIFE CENTRE

This facility was opened in 2010 and currently stands as one of the country's most popular attractions. This serves as a reserve for flightless Kiwi birds where hatching programs also take place. The entrance fee is NZ$35.

KAYAKING

Kayaking is a great activity to try at Franz Josef. The average rental charge per kayak is around NZ$60 while a kayaking tour costs about NZ$115. You can paddle across the lake and see glacial walls, the rainforest, and Kiwi sanctuaries along the way.

FISHING

There are several mountain lakes in Franz Josef and these offer excellent locations for fishing in the area. Anglers will surely love it here. There are also a number of slow-moving creeks where plenty of trout thrive.

HISTORIC SWINGING BRIDGE

There is a historic swinging bridge that can be walked to reach one of the main glaciers in the area. The walk will take about

15 minutes and is an activity that is ideal for the brave of heart as it can be extremely wobbly.

Chapter 5: Rotorua

Another popular New Zealand tourist destination is Rotorua. In the North Island, it is considered to be one of the most popular destinations to date. It is a great destination for those who are looking for some of the best nature walks on the country. It is also known for being a hub when it comes to experiencing the Maori culture.

It has geysers and spas and almost all attractions are a few streets apart. This is because Rotorua is a small town. Small but filled to the brim with adventure including excellent fare and ample nightlife.

Accommodations
In this part of the country, an average hostel room would cost around NZ$15-25 but travelers can choose to avail of private rooms for NZ$50-70 a night. There are hotels which cost NZ$70 to start. This can reach over NZ$100 a night depending on the style of hotel chosen and room size preferred.

Here are some of the best-rated accommodations in Rotorua:

REGENT OF ROTORUA
The regent of Rotorua is considered to be one of the best places to stay in the city owing to its location, facilities provided and also the service. You can avail many features here such as a spa and spend time in the restaurant that overlooks the sea. All in all, you are bound to have an amazing time at this hotel!

1191 Pukaki Street
00 64 7 808 1279

CEDARWOOD LAKESIDE

Located just 3 km from the domestic airport, this place is quite unique. It features a great view of the lake and provides you with a spacious suite. The suites are loaded with amenities such as television, Wi-Fi and kitchenettes that you can use to cook your own meals. They also come with separate living and dining rooms that you can use to avail a comfortable stay.

17 Holdens Avenue, Holdens Bay
00 64 7 808 1273

ARISTA CAPRI MOTEL

This is a 4-star hotel that serves the purpose of providing guests with a comfortable stay. The rooms are amazing and provide with some of the best views. They come equipped with all types of amenities such as television, Wi-Fi, minibar and other such that makes this place a great one to stay at. There are many common features that you can make use of including a hot tub.

290 Fenton Street
00 64 7 788 0006

Other options
- MALFROY MOTOR LODGE ROTORUA

51 Malfroy Road, Victoria
00 64 7 346 8053

- SOLITAIRE LODGE

16 Ronald Road, Lake Tarawera

- QUEST ROTORUA CENTRAL

1192 Hinemoa Street
00 64 7 788 0158

- **SILVER FERN ROTORUA**
326 Fenton Street

- **ARISTA OF ROTORUA (Formerly Cedar Lodge Motel)**
296 Fenton Street

- **HAMURANA LODGE**
415 Hamurana Road, RD7
00 64 7 808 2295

- **SPORT OF KINGS MOTEL**
6 Peace Street, Fenton Park
00 64 7 808 5053

Food and Beverage

Travelers that choose to dine in standard restaurants should expect to pay about NZ$20 per dish. It will be a good idea to cook at home as it will only cost about NZ$60-80 for a week's worth of meals. There are fast food joints in the area and a meal would typically cost NZ$8 and above.

Rotorua has a selection of small restaurants that all serve great food. Each one is unique in its own way.

Restaurants in Rotorua

Regent of Rotorua
The regent is a fairly new place and a great restaurant to eat at. You can find a delectable menu with some lip smacking dishes to savor. The place is very elegant and will ensure that you have a good time eating out. The breakfast here is quite popular as is the lunch. The entire menu has been redone

keeping in mind the traveller's palate and is sure to leave you feeling good about your meal.

1191 Pukaki St, +64 7 3484079

Solitaire lodge
The solitaire lodge is quite popular for its menu. They serve some authentic New Zealand cuisine that will satisfy your taste buds. The solitaire lodge is a high end staying option with some great views. But the restaurant is the main attraction here and has both travelers and locals smacking their lips. The place is quite reasonably priced and will not burn a hole in your pocket.

16 Ronald Rd, Lake Tarawera, +64 7 3628208

Indian star tandoori restaurant
Indian restaurants are quite popular in Rotorua. One such popular place is the Indian star tandoori restaurant that has won many awards for the delicious food that it serves. Right from the kebabs to the biryanis and the curries, there is a lot to choose from! The prices are pocket friendly, thereby making this a great place for family outings. Make sure you savor the sides here including the pickles and the chutneys!

1118 Tutanekai St - Eat Street +64 7 3436222

Nightclubs/bars in Rotorua

Kalah bar
Kalah bar is a great little place to party. There are live shows, DJs and parties to be a part of. The place is generally bustling with expats and locals all looking to have a good time. There is also a restaurant here where you can sample the buffet. You

will be able to delight your palate by sampling everything on the menu here.

11b Hall Rd, Ngongotaha, Rotorua

Teazer lounge
The Teazer nightclub is a popular bar in Rotorua. You can stay here till 3 am and party the night away. The place is known for its amazing cocktails. The food here is also recommended. The place provides you with some live entertainment and also shows sports events. The place is generally busy with locals and expats looking for a good time.

1207 Eruera Street, Rotorua

Hennessy's brew
Hennessy's brew is a good place for you to chill out and have a few drinks. The place is known for the beer that it serves and also the food. You will have a great time partying here and remain entertained. It is an Irish bar and the drinks and meals here are some of the most sought after in Rotorua.

1210 Tutanekai St, Rotorua 3010, New Zealand, +64 7-343 7901

Transportation
Because Rotorua is a small town, it would be best if you walked around and saw the city in its entirety. It is so small that walking from end to end would only take about twenty to thirty minutes. Those who want to take a nature walk or two around the hot springs and lake should expect about a two-hour walk. Cycling is the best form of transport in this part of the country and you should definitely try it out.

What to Do

ZORBING
A lot of backpackers go to Rotorua to go zorbing. A zorb is a giant ball made out of a see-through material then rolled downhill. One can imagine it as spinning round and round like clothes in a washing machine. One roll only takes a few seconds making it quite an expensive activity to engage in but worth trying.

HOT BATHS
The area is known for its hot sulfurous springs which make for a great day of relaxing. A popular spot here is a large Polynesian spa. You can pay the full-day fee and enjoy all amenities throughout the day. Access also includes free drinks. There is a heated pool by the Blue Baths as well.

SEE THE GEYSERS
Rotorua is known for being a geyser hotspot so plan to see these geysers when you visit the area. The geysers can be found in Te Puia. Apart from these, there are hot springs that are worth traveling to as well. The best thing about it is that you can walk around the area free of charge!

ROTORUA MUSEUM
An old bathhouse building was converted into the Rotorua museum. It houses exhibits reflecting the culture and history of Rotorua and its people. There are tons of Maori artifacts on display as well. The entrance fee is only NZ$20.

CANOPY TOUR
A canopy tour takes three hours to complete. It involves zip lining, swinging bridges, and going through a forest with half a century old trees. The fee is about NZ$140 per person but

worth trying out. The tour is best done with a small group of people.

WHAKA THERMAL RESERVE
Also make time to see the Whaka Thermal Reserve. It is an excellent facility that offers knowledge tours where you can learn not only about the geology of Rotorua but its natural history as well. There are guided tours for individuals and groups and fees vary accordingly.

WHAKAREWAREWA FOREST EXPLORATION
The Whakarewarewa Forest and is a 15-acre redwood grove where you can take part in nature walks, mountain bike rides, and other activities.

BURIED VILLAGE
The village was covered in ash when the nearby Mount Tarawera erupted in 1886 hence the name Buried Village. The site is home not only to the remains of the village but its people as well.

GOVERNMENT GARDENS
One of the most beautiful parks in the area is the Government Gardens. It is located near a golf course and the sports dome. This is where the Blue Baths can be found. The city museum is also within the vicinity.

ROTORUA LAKE
There is a beautiful lake in Rotorua. Actually, the town sits atop this lake. The perfect activity in this part of town is an afternoon cruise along the lake and a hike around the island. It's best to bring enough sunscreen, as the sun is pretty strong in New Zealand. A few minutes under the sun can mean intense sunburn.

MAORI CULTURAL IMMERSION

Rotorua is the best place to immerse oneself in Maori culture. There are cultural shows and educational tours that are worth joining. These will teach you a lot about the Maoris; who they are, how they live, what traditions they have, and so on and so forth. Cultural shows usually come packaged with a traditional dinner. One of the best educational tours is the local village tour.

AGRODOME

The Agrodome is an agricultural park filled with farm animals. It is where you can experience the local rural life as well. Farm tours are available and there is a free-fall experience simulator as well. The highest bungee jumping platform in the North Island can be found here.

14 LAKES

There are 14 lakes in the area and a tour is available if you want to traverse these lakes. A typical tour takes about ninety minutes to complete. It is also possible to take a car to visit the lakes one by one. Bring some fishing poles along.

Chapter 6: Wellington

The capital of New Zealand is Wellington and it is the third most populous urban dwelling in the country. It is an architectural powerhouse with eclectic offerings sure to impress travelers from around the globe. Aside from amazing daytime activities, Wellington is also the place to be for exciting nightlife, amazing food, and a magnificent view of a beautiful harbor.

Accommodations

Because it is where most of the action takes place, accommodations in Wellington can be pricier compared to other parts of the country. A hostel bed would cost about NZ$25-35 a night while private quarters would be priced around NZ$85. For hotel rooms, they can cost anywhere from NZ$80-140 a night.

Here are some of the best-rated accommodations in Wellington:

BOLTON HOTEL WELLINGTON
The Bolton hotel is a great staying option in Wellington. It provides with great views and spacious rooms. You can use the facilities provided by the hotel and have a great time. Some of these include great room service; spacious rooms and other amenities that make this place your number one choice. It is also very close to the city center.

12 Bolton Street, Lambton CBD
00 64 4 887 1871

MUSEUM ART HOTEL WELLINGTON

This is an art hotel located in Cable Street and makes for a quirky little place to stay at. The rooms are quite interesting and include a blend of contemporary and classics. The rooms all come with basic amenities such as television, Wi-Fi, minibars and refrigerator. You can also visit the fine dining restaurant that is attached to this hotel and savor some of their best dishes.

90 Cable Street, Te Aro

APOLLO LODGE MOTEL

Located quite close to the museum, this place is a great one to stay while in Wellington. The place provides for some interesting decor that is sure to delight you. The rooms all come with 1 to 3 bedrooms that are all equipped with basic amenities. The place is also quite close to the zoo and will make for a great place to stay with kids.

49 Majoribanks Street

Other options
- INTERCONTINENTAL WELLINGTON

2 Grey Street

00 1 877 859 5095

- BEST WESTERN WELLINGTON

17 - 19 Burgess Road, Johnsonville

- AT HOME WELLINGTON

Level 4, 181 Wakefield Street

00 64 4 887 1285

- OHTEL

66 Oriental Parade, Oriental Bay

- COPTHORNE HOTEL WELLINGTON BY ORIENTAL BAY
100 Oriental Parade, Oriental Bay

- CITYLIFE WELLINGTON
300 Lambton Quay

- RYDGES WELLINGTON
75 Featherston Street

Food and Beverage

A meal at a fancy restaurant starts at around NZ$25 and can go to as high as NZ$45 per plate. A weekly budget for groceries cost about NZ$60-90. Fast food areas are also available offering more affordable meal options to travelers. Meals here cost about NZ$8 to start.

Restaurants in Wellington

The restaurants in Wellington are all quite upscale and will serve out some great food.

Floriditas

Floriditas is a nice little upscale joint in Wellington that serves good food. They have a good menu going along with some great cupcakes. You can savor all of it in their cozy restaurant that recently had a face-lift. The wine served here is recommended and will go well with the menu.

Floriditas, 161 Cuba Street, Te Aro, Wellington City, 04 3812212

Matterhorn

The Matterhorn is a great little place where you can grab some amazing drinks. It is also a restaurant that serves great food. It is an upscale restaurant where you are sure to find some well made dishes. It will make for the perfect spot for a Sunday brunch with family and friends.

Matterhorn, 106 Cuba Street, Te Aro, Wellington City

Fidel's café

If you are in the mood for some good food without too much fuss then Fidel's café is the one for you. The place is quite rustic and serves out some amazing food. You can select from a large menu here, mostly consisting of light bites. The coffee that is served here is also pretty famous and a must try.

Fidel's, 234 Cuba Street, Te Aro, Wellington City, 04 8016868

Loretta

Loretta is a great place to have a sumptuous meal. They keep changing the menu here to keep it interesting. Right from the waffles to the amazing fresh lunches, everything served here is superb. The restaurant tries to focus on the seasonal produce and comes up with a menu that suits the particular season. The interiors of this place are quite interesting and will delight you.

Loretta, 181 Cuba Street, Te Aro, Wellington City, 04 3842213

Nightclubs/bars in Wellington

Motel bar

Motel bar is a great little hangout place in Wellington. Here, you can select from a variety of island-style cocktails all served in tiki glasses. The place can be considered a tropical heaven with the food being quite good.

Motel Bar, Level 1, 2 Forresters Lane, Te Aro, Wellington City, 04 3849084

Mac's bar

Mac's bar is a great little place for you to try out some drinks. The food here is great too and will leave wanting more. Mac's bar has a nice atmosphere and an interesting décor. You will be transported back in time and be able to savor authentic Kiwi food.

Mac's Restaurant and Brew Bar, 4 Taranaki Street, Wellington Central, Wellington City, 04 3812282

Foxglove

Foxglove located on the waterfront is a great place to visit. The bar cum restaurant is a great place for you to enjoy a meal and a drink. The chefs at Foxglove are all well trained and serve up an amazing meal each time. The drinks are also great and will please even the fussiest person's palate. The decor here is amazing and exudes an old-world charm.

Foxglove Bar & Kitchen, 33 Queens Wharf, Wellington Central, Wellington City, 04 4609410

Transportation

The city is home to the Metlink. The Metlink is an interlinked bus network that offers access not only to traditional buses but trains, ferries, cable cars, and trolley buses as well. The costs vary depending on which mode of transport is chosen but the fees are fairly reasonable and transport time is quite fast.

What to Do

There are different activities that you can engage in when you visit the country's capital. There are offerings for travelers of varying interests making it an excellent destination for adults, the elderly, and children.

ASIAN FOOD TRIP

Although it might seem puzzling to have to travel all the way to New Zealand to eat Asian food, there is reasonable logic behind it. You can partake in some of the finest Asian food in New Zealand in Wellington. Not only do these meals come aplenty but also they are rather cheap which means you can have a full belly without a blown budget.

WELLINGTON ZOO

For more animal sightings, do visit the Wellington zoo, the oldest zoo in the country. It houses different native wildlife from Africa and Asia. Entry costs NZ$32 per person.

SAINT PAUL'S

Saint Paul's Cathedral is made using native timbers. It is an excellent example of colonial Gothic architecture.

NATIONAL ARCHIVES

It would be mentally engaging to see some of the country's most valued documents on display. Do pay the National Archives a visit. Here is where you will see the treaty of Waitangi. It was signed way back in 1893. There is also the Women's Suffrage Petition.

BEEHIVE AND PARLIAMENT HOUSE

In Wellington, there is a government building called The Beehive and beside it is the House of Parliament. These structures are only a short distance away from one of the main train stations in the city so they are pretty easy to find. Not all parts are accessible to the public but the main halls are by means of a guided tour. The tour is free and you can even watch the members of parliament in action.

LOOKOUTS

The area, despite being a city center, has a hilly backdrop. This makes for excellent lookout points scattered across Wellington. Climbing one of these hills offers travelers an excellent view of the city and its surroundings. Other ways of reaching the top of these hills include access by bus, cable car, or bicycles.

BOTANICAL GARDENS

For a day of rest and relaxation, a stroll through the local botanic gardens will do you a lot of good. It is accessible by cable car. Initial access is through Lambton Quay. It only takes several minutes to reach the gardens from this point. Aside from the breathtaking views, you can enjoy a picnic or two not to mention marvel at the wonderful array of flowers.

NEW ZEALAND FILM ARCHIVE

The film archive was established in the early eighties and it is a library that safe keeps over thirty thousand movies. These movies can be watched free of charge.

SEVENS

The Sevens is New Zealand's official rugby tournament. It is held annually, every February, and takes place at the Westpac Stadium.

KARORI WILDLIFE SANCTUARY

The Karori Wildlife Sanctuary is a conservation facility that serves as a reservation for endangered New Zealand wildlife. This includes species such as the Kiwi, the Weka birds, the Kakas, and the Saddlebacks.

There are over twenty-two miles of walking trails and it also boasts a goldmine dating back to the 19th century. Those who want to witness the beauty of nature and see the native wildlife should definitely pay the sanctuary a visit.

MUSEUM OF WELLINGTON CITY
This museum charges no admission fee. It chronicles the maritime history of New Zealand.

TE PAPA
Te Papa is considered as a national museum. It exhibits colonial and Maori history and offers displays on New Zealand geology. It is a great museum for children and is free to enter.

CARTER OBSERVATORY
The Carter Observatory is located near the botanic gardens. It is a dome structure that houses a planetarium. It is an excellent location for stargazing as well. During the day, you can take a look at the exhibits, watch shows on the cosmos, or treat yourself to novelties in the gift shop.

ZEALANDIA
Zealandia is another wildlife sanctuary. It is located by the west side of Wellington and houses several bird species. Guided tours are available but visitors can walk freely if they prefer.

Chapter 7: Bay of Islands

One of New Zealand's most popular destinations is the Bay of Islands that can be found on the northern part of the country. It is known for its lengthy shoreline offering miles of beach access not to mention surrounding islands totaling 144. Some of the main activities locals and tourists engage in are sailing and big-game fishing. Cruises, kayaking trips, and swimming with dolphins are other popular attractions here.

Accommodations

Hostels are affordable means of accommodation as dorm rooms only cost about NZ$15-30 per night. The going rate for private rooms is NZ$50-80. Do consider staying in the Paihia area, the main town, if you plan on booking a hostel, as establishments are all located on the main street. As for the budget hotels, their prices depend on seasonality that peaks during January, which is the start of summer. Depending on the time of year, rooms may cost anywhere from NZ$60-160 per night.

Here are some of the best-rated accommodations in the Bay of Islands:

RUSSELL COTTAGES

Russell cottages is a great choice for those looking to stay in Bay of Islands for a short time. This place is crafted to suit the likes of those that are looking for basic amenities and nothing too fancy. The place provides for clean and spacious rooms where you can have a great time. You can make use of their quality room service. The place is quite close to the city center.

16 Chapel Street, Russell

BREAKWATER MOTEL

The breakwater is a sophisticated motel that you can consider to stay at in Bay of Islands. It provides for some great views and is located quite close to the museum. The rooms all feature basic amenities such as television, minibar, refrigerator etc. You can make use of the hot tub and barbeque that is a must try at this hotel.

1 Bayview Road, Paihia

HANANUI LODGE MOTEL

The hahanui is located at a 3-minute walk from the museum. The hotel provides some great rooms that are comfortable to stay in. there are a lot of facilities available inside the rooms including television, air conditioner and a kitchenette where you can prepare your food. You can also request for additional beds here.

4 York Street, P.O. Box 16, Russell

Other options

- PIONEER WATERFRONT APARTMENTS
44 Marsden Road, Northland, Paihia
00 64 9 887 9734

- COOK'S LOOKOUT MOTEL
9 Causeway Road, P.O. Box 380, Paihia
00 64 9 887 8312

- KAURI PARK MOTEL
512 Kerikeri Road, Kerikeri
00 64 9 407 7629

- WOODLANDS MOTEL AND CONFERENCE VENUE
126 Kerikeri Rd, Kerikeri

- OUTRIGGER MOTEL
45 Williams Road, P.O. Box 239, Paihia

- KERIKERI PARK MOTEL
494b Kerikeri Road, Kerikeri
00 64 9 887 9824

- PEARL OF THE BAY (Formerly Bali Hai Motel)
8-10 Coutts Avenue, Paihia

Food and Beverage

An average rate of NZ$30 per meal can be expected from the local restaurants here. Nicer restaurants charge about NZ$45-60 per plate. If you want to do your own cooking, set a weekly budget of NZ$50-75. Popular here are the local pizza and fish and chip joints that offer NZ$9 meals.

Bay of islands has a great collection of restaurants. The food out there is quite insane.

Restaurants in Bay of Islands

Gables
Gables is an amazing restaurant that serves up Kiwi classics. Right from lamb to seafood to venison, the food here is simply amazing. The restaurant is set in an 1847 building and exudes an old world charm. You can sit by the window to catch a glimpse of the views outside. The food served here is made from fresh produce that is sourced locally. The bar here is also quite popular and serves up some great drinks.
19 The Strand, Bay of Islands & Northland, New Zealand

Wharepuke

The Wharepuke serves great Thai food. So if you are in the mood for some Asian cuisine then you can head over to Wharepuke on Friday nights. You will have the chance to enjoy a delectable meal and treat your senses. You can enjoy some live jazz on Sunday afternoons while savoring dishes from the amazing menu.

190 Kerikeri Road, Bay of Islands & Northland, New Zealand

A deco

A deco is a restaurant that serves up amazing food that focuses on the local produce. It sets the menu based on the season and whatever vegetable is trending. The place is set in an old world villa that is bound to please you. A deco is consistently voted as the number 1 restaurant in the Northland owing to the great food and super drinks that it has on offer. This is a must visit for you when you travel to the bay of islands.

70 Kamo Rd Bay of Islands & Northland, New Zealand

Nightclubs/bars in Bay of islands

Jimmy Cook's bar

Jimmy Cook's bar offers you an amazing place to cool yourself off. The place serves some authentic New Zealand wines that will leave you smacking your lips. There are also many cocktails available here and a range of craft beers. The al fresco area here is superb, where you can chill by the beach with a drink in hand and take in the majestic views.

Tau Henare Drive PO Box 150 Paihia, 0200 New Zealand, +64 9 402 7411

Alongside bar

Situated over the water, alongside bar is a fairly new place that is gaining immense popularity. It serves amazing drinks and also offers great food. You simply must try out the wines here that pair well with the food. The rum collection is also quite popular and will satisfy your palate.

69 Marsden Road or PO Box 433, Paihia, Bay of Islands, Northland, New Zealand, 09 402 6220

<u>35 degrees south</u>
35 degrees south is a bar that is set on the water and makes for a comfortable bar. You can enjoy the views and soak in the atmosphere. The place offers mouth-watering treats that are all designed to go with the delicious drinks that range from wines to beers. You can enjoy a cozy meal here and wash it down with a tasty cocktail.

Transportation
Because of its extended shoreline, the best way to navigate the Bay of Islands is by ferry service. A local ferry operates daily between Russel and Paihia with each trip lasting about 15 minutes costing NZ$6 per way (NZ$12 round trip). Bus access is also available and only costs NZ$1 from Auckland but advanced bookings are necessary so that you are assured a seat. Last-minute bookings will set you back about NZ$30 for a one-way ride.

What to Do
The Bay of Islands is an excellent place to visit for those who enjoy the sand, sea, and sun:

<u>BEACHES</u>
There are plenty of beaches to choose from in the Bay of Islands all of which can be found along a lengthy stretch of land. There are public access beaches and those that are more secluded in nature. It is best to come early especially during

the summer months as these tend to fill up fast. Aside from taking a dip, you can relax and lounge under the warm sun.

RAINBOW FALLS
Kerikeri offers access to Rainbow Falls, which can be reached after a three-mile hike. It was named Rainbow Falls because rainbows would form at the pool by the base of the waterfall.

Before heading to the falls however, it will be a good idea to visit The Parrot Place. This is an aviary where 300 bird species can be found. The facility offers live interactions with the birds where you can hold and feed them. A great activity for kids, entry costs NZ$10 per person.

HISTORICAL SITES
Several historical landmarks can be found in the area starting with the Waitangi Treaty Grounds, which is reflective of the country's past. The Treaty of Waitangi, the country's most important document, was signed here in 1840. It was a treaty between the British and Maori chiefs and gave life to modern day New Zealand.

Another excellent location to include in the itinerary is the Pompallier House. Regular tours are available here. It is a French Catholic mission house established in the 19th century and now stands as a museum. The entry fee is NZ$10. Inside, you will see the factory, tannery, and printing press that were owned and operated by the missionaries back in the day.

There is also the Russell Museum where Maori art and artifacts are displayed.

SAILING

Sailing is an extremely popular activity in this part of the country. There are plenty of sailboats in the area which can be rented for a day for about NZ$100. The great thing about sailing trips is that travelers can also choose to engage in side trips. They can go scuba diving or swimming with the dolphins. Amazing coral reefs and rich marine life make for excellent diving while the latter, on a chartered tour, costs about NZ$100 per person.

TREKKING

The local weather is close to perfect making trekking an excellent activity on the Bay of Islands. You can enjoy the beautiful scenery and engage in a wide selection of guided hikes. You can also ride a horse along the trails.

FISHING

Big-game fishermen will love it here, as there is an abundance of marlin, snappers, and kingfish. NZ$100 is equivalent to a half-day chartered excursion. Since the trip will only take a short amount of time, it would be best to make a trip to Cape Reinga as well.

For NZ$145, you can reach the northernmost tip of New Zealand. Here is where the ancient Puketi Kauri Forest can be found. It is known not only for sand boarding but its line of massive trees as well.

Chapter 8: Nelson

If you're looking for a sunny place in New Zealand then head on off to Nelson, a city filled with amazing pubs, cafes, and restaurants – it is the ultimate foodie's delight. A heavily mountainous area, it is the perfect destination for those interested in a good hike. Several beaches can also be found in Nelson and of course, there is the Abel Tasman National Park.

Tourists often make the mistake of overlooking the area but given enough time, about two to three days, one will discover an amazing locale with plenty of exciting activities to engage in with some of the friendliest and outgoing locals in the country.

Accommodations

You can choose to stay in hostels with beds ranging from NZ$25-30. Private rooms are also available and cost about NZ$65 a night. A number of budget hotels can be found in the area as well with rooms costing NZ$75 per night.

Here are some of the best-rated accommodations in Nelson:

ARCADIA MOTEL

The Arcadia 4 star hotel that is located 5 kms from the airport. It is quite close to the city center and will make for a great option to stay at. The place comes with several amenities such as flat screen televisions, microwaves, minibar and refrigerators. There are also sofas and a dining set available in every room where you can relax and enjoy.

36 Golf Road, Tahunanui
00 64 4 488 7231

THE SAILS NELSON
The Sails is a great little place for you to stay when in Nelson. The rooms here come with all the basic amenities including television, minibar, refrigerator etc. You can use the amenities provided by the place such as the amazing breakfast selection that will satisfy you thoroughly.

7 Trafalgar Street
00 64 3 667 1553

CENTURY PARK MOTOR LODGE
Lying just 5 minutes from the nearest bus stop and 8 km away from the waterfront, this hotel is a great choice for all those that wish to stay close to the center of the city. The place offers some amazing food that you can savor. It also has some great room service on offer that you can enjoy during your stay.

197 Rutherford Street
00 64 3 668 0697

Other options
- ALOHA LODGE
19 Beach Road, Tahunanui
00 64 9 887 8410

- DELORENZOS STUDIO APARTMENTS
43 - 55 Trafalgar Street

- DRIFTWOOD MOTELS
21 Muritai Street, Tahunanui

- CHELSEA PARK MOTOR LODGE
214 Rutherford Street
00 64 3 546 6494

- PALAZZO MOTOR LODGE
159 Rutherford Street
00 64 3 668 0651

- BAY CREST MOTOR LODGE
87 Golf Road, Tahunanui
00 64 3 588 0045

- HARBOURSIDE MOTOR LODGE
4 Duncan Street

Food and Beverage

On average, a restaurant meal will set you back about NZ$30. It will be a good idea to home-cook your meals as doing so will only cost about NZ$50-75 per week. Fast food establishments offer meals at NZ$8-15 per set. As for the local bars, drinks normally cost NZ$7 each.

Nelson has its own collection of restaurants and bars, each of which is pretty unique.

Restaurants in Nelson

River kitchen

The river kitchen is a cozy little place located on the Maitai River. It offers an amazing menu full of top class dishes. The fish and chips here is a must try and so is the rib eye steak. The dining room here is bright and open and provides for a great atmosphere. You can savor the burger here that comes with homemade buns and pickles. The breakfast served here is also pretty delectable.

River Kitchen, 81 Trafalgar Street, Nelson, New Zealand, +64 3-548 1180

Broccoli row

If you are looking for great vegetarian options then broccoli row is the one for you. The restaurant was opened after popular demand and serves up some amazing vegetarian recipes. It also comes up with some non-vegetarian dishes every now and then that are just as amazing as the veg options. The desserts here are also recommended and will leave you feeling great after a hearty meal.

Broccoli Row, Cnr of Trafalgar Street and Halifax Street East, Nelson, New Zealand, +64 3-548 9621

The Styx

The Styx is a great little restaurant to try out while you are at Nelson. It is a double decker restaurant cum bar that serves some amazing seafood. The scallop carbonara is a must try, as is the calamari salad. The place also offers some amazing views of the bay that is sure to make you happy. You can make it to the café at lunchtime to catch a glimpse of the sunset here.

The Styx Kitchen and Bar, 272 Wakefield Quay, Nelson, New Zealand, +64 3-548 1075

The Indian café

The Indian café is a great little place for you to avail a hearty meal. The place is now very popular owing to the amazing food that it offers. You are sure to find a meal that has been prepared using the freshest ingredients. The curries here are simply superb and a must try. The fish curry is a class apart and will leave you licking your fingers.

The Indian Café, 94 Collingwood Street, Nelson, New Zealand, +64 3-548 4089

Nightclubs/bars in Nelson

Little Rock bar and nightclub

The Little Rock bar and nightclub is a swanky little place for you to hit post after hours. The place serves some amazing cocktails and drinks and also has a good food menu. The place is generally bustling with young partygoers looking to have a good time. The place has karaoke nights on Wednesdays and a DJ night on Fridays.

165 Bridge Street, Nelson 7010, (03) 5468800

Craft beer depot

Nelson is known as the craft beer destination of the world. It brews up some of the best beer in the world and is known for its strong and unique taste. Once you sample the beer here, you are sure to come back for more! The craft beer depot is one such place that serves some of the best beer in the world. You can drink to your heart's content as the place serves up some of the best beer in the world.

Achilles Ave (Wakatu Square), Nelson, 03 548-2126

McCashin's brewery

McCashin's brewery is a must visit in Nelson as it serves up amazing crafted beer. The food menu is also great here, as the place is known to serve out lip smacking snacks. You can also try out their coffee, which is regarded as one of the best in Nelson. The place is open 7 days a week, 365 days a year, making it one of the most visited bars in Nelson.

660 Main Road Stoke, Nelson, 03 547 0329

Transportation

The best option for transport around Nelson is the local bus service. The main terminal can be found in Wakatu Square. It is located between Bridge Street and Ajax Avenue. If you are staying in a local hostel, you can inquire about bike rentals as many offer this service for a minimal fee and it is a great way to see the sights.

What to Do

Nelson offers plenty of activities that won't burn a hole in your wallet:

ART GALLERIES/MUSEUMS

If you are a fan of fine art, a trip to the Suter Art Gallery should be included in your itinerary. It is the third largest art museum in the country and showcases the works of Kiwi artists. The predominant medium highlighted here is paint. To see more cultural art pieces, you have to visit the Nelson Provincial Museum.

MIYAZU JAPANESE GARDEN

This is perfect for those who want to relax with a quiet and calming stroll. The traditional Japanese garden is an excellent venue for travelers who want to engage in some contemplative meditation. It is best to visit during spring as cherry blossoms are in full bloom.

ABEL TASMAN NATIONAL PARK

Hiking at Abel Tasman is free. There are trails of different difficulty levels. Be sure to pack some insect repellent, as sand flies are known to frequent the area. Expect a relatively cool environment as the area is lined with trees and ferns.

On the other side of the park are several blue water beaches, some of the most beautiful in New Zealand. The best way to explore this area is with a kayak, as it will allow you to pass through the little coves and narrow water paths.

FOUNDERS HERITAGE PARK

There is another park, a smaller one, which can be found by the city center. It is where you will find a replica of their historical village. Surrounding the compound are small cafes and breweries plus a couple of small-scale museums. There is a local brewery that crafts some of the finest beer in the country. It is organic and worth every drop.

GLASSBLOWING

Glassblowing is another activity that you can try out when in Nelson. The Hoglund Art Glass Studio offers tours to those who want an inside look into the art of glassblowing. The craftsmen here are internationally renowned and have spent decades perfecting their art. Aside from the actual workroom where live demonstrations are held, there is also a small gallery where various pieces are displayed.

SHARK CLUB

A game of pool at the Shark Club will be a great experience. The Shark Club is a small local pub that the locals absolutely adore. The food is excellent but quite cheap so you can indulge in some of the best pub fare around. There are a number of pool tables inside which can be accessed free of charge during happy hour.

MAPUA LEISURE PARK

A short distance from Nelson is where you will find Mapua; a commercial outdoor park that opens every February until

March. It offers several swimming pools, sporting areas, saunas, spas, and a café.

NELSON MARKET
Do explore the Nelson Market as well. You can find it at the car park of Montgomery Square. It is a Saturday market that is known for its amazing offerings of fresh organic produce: fruits, vegetables, and flowers. You will find stalls that sell locally farmed salmon as well. At one end of the market are merchants selling various crafts including jewelry, weaving, woodturning, silk paintings, and pottery.

WINE TOUR
Wine aficionados will love the local wine tour. There are over twenty actively operating wineries in the area offering a perfect end to a day's worth of hiking and kayaking. In Nelson, the specialty is white wine so be sure to try a bottle or two. Take some home with you if you like.

WOW
If you are a fan of fine clothes, see to it that you visit the World of Wearable Art and Collectible Cars or WOW. This is a museum that is quite unique as it showcases the works of local but internationally recognized fashion designers.

FAREWELL SPLIT
Finally, there is Farewell Split. It can be found on the northern tip of the island. It is similar to a sandbar but is made from a strip of natural land running into the sea. On this piece of land lies a bird sanctuary. Bird lovers should definitely arrange a 4WD tour.

Chapter 9: Taupo

There is a place in New Zealand that is reflective of Queenstown culture, only quieter and it is called Taupo. It is found on the shores of its namesake lake. It is known for being a party island in the South Island and offers numerous activities from hiking to fishing. There is a popular jump-off point here, the Tongario Alpine Crossing, which is world-renowned.

A short distance from the main city is the impressive Huka Falls, which can be visited for nature walks and cozy picnics. Aside from the excellent scenery, Taupo is also known for its good fare and very hospitable locals. Most visitors who travel here end up staying longer than they originally planned.

Accommodations
Usually, hostel dorm beds go for about NZ$25-30 per night per person while average rooms in these facilities cost NZ$55 on average. There are hotels that offer rooms at prices averaging NZ$85 and above.

Here are some of the best-rated accommodations in Taupo:

SACRED WATERS TAUPO LUXURY APARTMENTS
This is a luxury accommodation situated on the lakefront. It lies 9 kms away from the Huka falls and 1 km from the hot springs. It provides 1 to 4 bedroom suites that make for comfortable stay. You can enjoy the outdoor pool here and also the fitness center that is complimentary. The whirlpool bath is also a great feature to enjoy here.

221 - 225 Lake Terrace
00 64 7 808 3140

THE REEF RESORT

This is a fancy little resort that you can stay at in Taupo. The elegant studio style suites consist of several amenities including television. Minibar, refrigerator etc. there are also other amenities like the hot tub and the barbeque that you can sample at the restaurant. If you choose the 3 room deluxe package then you can have all of these in the comfort of your own room.

219 Lake Terrace, Town Center

CLEARWATER MOTOR LODGE

The Clearwater motor lodge is a great place to consider as it provides some amazing views. You can enjoy the many facilities here that are available here. The suites are all clean and well maintained and will provide you with basic amenities such as television, minibar, refrigerator etc.

229 Lake Terrace
00 64 7 788 4061

Other options
- ANCHORAGE RESORT
State Highway 1, Two Mile Bay
00 64 7 808 3122

- ASCOT MOTOR INN
70 Rifle Range Road
00 64 7 808 1224

- THE COTTAGE MEWS MOTEL TAUPO
311 Lake Terrace
00 64 7 808 3131

- WAIMAHANA LUXURY LAKESIDE APARTMENTS

2 Lowell Place off Lake Terrace corner of Lowell Road and Lake Terrace

- BAYCREST LODGE

79 Mere Road

00 64 7 808 1268

- THE PILLARS RETREAT

7 Deborah Rise, Bonshaw Park

- GABLES LAKEFRONT MOTEL

130 Lake Terrace

00 64 7 808 5060

Food and Beverage

City restaurants offer fine fare at about NZ$30 a plate. A week's worth of groceries here would cost NZ$54-77 making it a perfect alternative for travelers working with a strict budget. Fast food restaurants can also be found with ease where meals cost anywhere from NZ$7-15 per meal.

Taupo has amazing restaurants that serve great food. Travelers will have a great time savoring all the food on offer in this town.

Restaurants in Taupo

L'arte café

L'arte café has consistently been voted as one of Taupo's top restaurants. It also happens to be one of the 10 must visit places in New Zealand. The place has some amazing pieces of art that are quite intriguing. You will have a great time going through all of it while gorging on some great food. The place also offers some amazing coffee and a selection of local beers, wines and homemade breads.

255 Mapara road, Acacia bay, Taupo, +6473782962

Storehouse
The Storehouse is a food joint that is not to be missed in Taupo. The place serves up some amazing tapas that is sure to delight you. The coffee served here is also quite popular and invites a big crowd. The place serves tapas from Thursday to Sunday and you might want to reserve a table as it fills up quite fast. The interiors here are quite unique and you will have a fun time going through all the stuff that is on display.

14 Runanga St, Taupo

Victoria's café
Victoria's café is a must visit in Taupo as it serves out some amazing food. The place is open everyday and is known for its unique whiskey club. The restaurant serves out great food in the mornings and evenings and is savored by both locals and tourists. You can have a great time here with family and friends as you dig into some of the best food in Taupo.

127 Tongario Street, Taupo, 073767310

Nightclubs/bars in Taupo

Mulligans public house
Mulligans public house is a great little bar that you can visit to savor some amazing drinks. The place can be seen as a good one to host parties for your friends and family. You can taste the menu here and savor the local brews. The place, like most others, is open 7 days a week thereby allowing you to step in at

any time of the day. The place is famous for its quiz nights and you are sure to

15 Tongariro St Taupo 3330, 07 376 9100

Plateau bar and restaurant

If you are looking for some amazing craft beer then it is a must for you to visit plateau bar and restaurant. The place serves up some great beer that you can have with the delectable food that is served here. The atmosphere at the bar is quite amazing and is located on the shore of lake Taupo. The place is known for its fresh menu and the lamb and beef served here is a must try! You can throw a party here and have a fun time with friends and family.

64 Tuwharetoa St Taupo 3330, 07 377 2425

Pub and grub

Pub and grub serves not just great beer but also some amazing food. In fact, the place is a must visit for all those looking for a good place to eat some amazing food. The drinks are not limited to beer alone and you can try out the cocktails as well. The place offers some amazing discounts for friends and family as well.

4 Roberts St Taupo 3330, 07 378 0555

Transportation

Taupo has an official bus line, which is called the Taupo Connector. A single journey ticket will cost NZ$1.50 while round trip fare costs approximately NZ$2.50.

What to Do

There are plenty of different activities that can be enjoyed by those visiting Taupo and here are some of them.

TONGARIRO ALPINE CROSSING
One of the best activities to engage in in Taupo is to take a hike around the Tongariro Alpine Crossing as this is considered to be the best hiking area in all of New Zealand. The crossing is where Mordor from the Lord of the Rings movie franchise was filmed.
A typical walk around the crossing would last for twelve miles. There are parts that are easy to traverse while others are steeper. It gives visitors access to the local forests, mountains, and volcanoes. It's best to reserve a full day for this, as there are plenty of things to see.

TANDEM SKYDIVING
Another excellent activity here is tandem skydiving. If skydiving alone was exciting, sharing the experience with a friend is even more exhilarating! Taupo is known to provide one of the best skydiving settings in the country as Lake Taupo offers an amazing view as jumpers leap from a height of 12,000 feet. The cost of tandem skydiving is about NZ$250-300 per jump.

TURANGI
Swimming in Turangi is something you should not miss out on. Turangi is a river that has an area where hot springs can be found. It offers an excellent opportunity for rest and relaxation not to mention some fine swimming time. During the winter months, it is an excellent destination for those who want to stay warm.

HUKA FALLS

The Huka Falls is one of the fastest moving waterfalls in all of New Zealand where the water flows so fast that it is able to retain its pristine blue color. Most visitors have compared its shade with that of an iceberg. The water here is different because it does not have too much oxygen and this is one of the things that contribute to its iceberg-like appearance.

BUNGEE JUMPING

Adrenalin junkies will enjoy bungee jumping in Taupo. Compared with other offerings in the country, the prices charged here are quite reasonable.

EXPLORE

The city is home to a number of nature trails and scenic routes that can be explored for free so be sure to take advantage of them. You can go on hikes, visit the Taupo Lake, trek through the mountains, and engage in some fishing.

SATURDAY MARKET

There is a well-known Saturday market setup by Riverside Park where the freshest produce can be found. It takes place every week and also offers booths that sell local crafts. There are times when they hold art exhibitions here and it is a must-see. Again, there is no admission fee.

GREAT LAKE CENTER

The Great Lake Center is the local multi-purpose structure in Taupo. It is often used as the venue not only for conventions and exhibitions but various performances as well. For travelers interested in a different kind of activity, this is the place to be.

LAKE TAUPO

The island's namesake, this lake, is the area's primary tourist attraction. There is a boardwalk where you will find some of the best restaurants in the area. It is a place where you can also engage in some hiking.

Especially during the months of summer, this area is flocked to by visitors because of activities such as trout fishing, sailing, boating, and jet skiing. Spending a full day here may not even be enough especially for a first-time visitor.

LAKE TAUPO MUSEUM AND ART GALLERY

For an inside look into the local culture, there is a museum and gallery, which can be found within city limits. It is located by Story Place behind the Great Lake Center. There are exhibits on Maori culture and the history of Taupo. Information on the local volcanoes and their activity can also be found here. It also features the work of local New Zealander artists.

SKIING AT TUROA

The Turoa is a skiing area that is located inside the Tongariro National Park. It is an excellent skiing venue for skiers of varying expertise. They offer gear for rent and retail. There is a ski school for children and there are ski guides everywhere!

JET BOATING AT WAIKATO

Waikato is the largest river in the country. It is also the best spot in New Zealand for some serious boating. Jet boating makes a simple activity extremely thrilling as boaters get to cruise through the river at rapid speeds.

MOUNT TAUHARA

Mountaineers should not pass up the opportunity to climb Mount Tauhara, which can be found on the eastern part of Taupo. It offers an opportunity for an easy but rewarding climb. The views from the top are truly astonishing.

BUTCHER'S POOL

Set in the middle of nature, the Butcher's Pool is a natural thermal spring that offers an excellent place for rest and relaxation. The best part about it is that it rarely has crowds.

Chapter 10: Christchurch

When someone mentions the garden city, chances are they are talking about Christchurch. It is an area in New Zealand that is known for its beautifully sculpted gardens and parks. These were designed to highlight the elegance of the Victorian age.

It is the designated backpacker center of the country, hence the large student-visitor population. Humorously, the local government even designated someone to be its wizard. An earthquake back in 2011 caused severe damage to Christchurch but the city has slowly rebuilt itself from the wreckage.

Accommodations

It is more affordable to stay in this part of the country. Hostels charge around NZ$25-35 per bunk while private rooms can be rented out for only NZ$50-65. Hotels cost around NZ$60-120 a night on average. The prices usually vary depending on the season.

Here are some of the best-rated accommodations in Christchurch:

TUSCANA MOTOR LODGE

This place is a great one to stay at. It is quite close to the city center. You can enjoy your stay here and make use of all the amenities on offer. The Tuscana motor lodge is a great option for all those that are staying for a short time. The place is quite quaint and will offer some much needed peace.

74 Bealey Avenue

MERIVALE MANOR

Just 3 minutes away from the closest bus stop, this is a good place to consider for you to stay. You can make use of the many free facilities here including the parking, laundry and the breakfast. All of here will make your stay well worth it and allow you to enjoy your time. The rooms are quite spacious and come with basic amenities, such as television, minibar etc.

122 Papanui Road, Merivale
00 64 3 668 0621

AMROSS COURT MOTOR LODGE

Just 7 minutes away from the bus stop, this is a good place to stay at. The rooms are cozy and come with many basic amenities such as flat screen television, DVD players, 1 to 2 bedroom suites, living rooms and dining spaces. The best part about this place is that allows pets, which is a great utility for all those that wish to travel with their pets.

61 Bealey Avenue
00 64 3 377 1554

Other options
- THE GEORGE CHRISTCHURCH

50 Park Terrace
00 64 3 668 1255

- AIRPORT PALMS MOTEL

56 Roydvale Avenue, Burnside
00 64 3 669 4648

- LORENZO MOTOR LODGE

36 Riccarton Road
00 64 3 668 0624

- CENTREPOINT ON COLOMBO MOTEL
859 Colombo Street

- COMMODORE AIRPORT HOTEL CHRISTCHURCH (Formerly Copthorne Hotel Commodore Christchurch Airport)
449 Memorial Avenue
00 64 3 668 0689

- AMORE MOTOR LODGE
168 Riccarton Road, Riccarton

- THE CLASSIC VILLA
17 Worcester Boulevard, Christchurch Arts Centre

Food and Beverage

A pretty decent meal out of a standard restaurant will cost NZ$18 on average. If you opt for self-cooking means, prepare to set a weekly budget of NZ$75-90. Cheaper alternatives in the forms of sandwiches or fast food options are available at about NZ$8-12 per meal.

Restaurants in Christchurch are quite good. You will have a great time exploring the food on offer here.

Restaurants in Christchurch

Strawberry fare

Strawberry fare serves amazing organic food that is fresh and simple. The food is crafted to suit the palate of the individual, which makes this a great place to have your meals. You can try out the breakfast at this place, which is quite unique and sumptuous. The corn and capsicum fritters are a winner and a must try at this joint. The interior at the place is quite classy with a black and white monochrome theme.

19 Bealey Ave, Christchurch Central, Christchurch, New Zealand, +64 3-365 4665

The old vicarage

The old vicarage is a beautiful little restaurant that makes for a must visit in Christchurch. The restaurant here serves great food. You can enjoy it in the elegant dining area or also in the alfresco area of the hotel. You must try the smoked fish and mussel chowder served here as well as the shiitake oysters. You can wash it all down with some beer and wine. It will make for the perfect place for a Sunday brunch with friends.

335 Halswell Rd, Halswell, Christchurch, New Zealand, +64 3-322 1224

Gustav's kitchen and wine bar

Gustav's kitchen and bar serves some amazing food that you can savor any day of the week. The place offers some amazing wine and brews that are all meant to complement the food here. You can try the mackerel escabeche here, which is well known for its amazing taste. The grilled quinoa is also a must try at the restaurant.

3 Garlands Rd, Woolston, Christchurch, New Zealand, +64 3-389 5544

Nightclubs/bars in Christchurch

Club 604

Club 604 is the party destination in Christchurch. The place is generally full of young partygoers shaking a leg on the dance floor. The drinks here are great and you can also savor some of the snacks. The laser show here is quite awesome and you can expect to have a great time. There are two bars available here along with gaming machines that are bound to keep you busy for long.

604 Ferry Road, Woolston, Christchurch, 384 1500

Cargo bar

If you are looking for a unique experience, then cargo bar is a must visit in Christchurch. The place has been carved out of cargo containers and makes for a great place to chill. The food served here is delicious. The music and drinks are also top notch and will ensure that you have a great time. You can visit the place with friends and party the night away!

359 Lincoln Road, Addington, Christchurch, 03 338 9107

Sullivan's Irish pub

The Sullivan's Irish pub should be a priority when you visit Christchurch. You will have the chance to savor some amazing beer and also tuck into some sumptuous snacks. You can grab a seat and savor some good brew or dance the night away. The place is generally bustling with people looking to have a great time with friends and family.

291 Lincoln Rd, Addington, Christchurch, 03 338 8300

Transportation

A must-do when in Christchurch is to ride its tramway. The tram has been running for decades and operations were only halted when the 2011 earthquake struck. A ticket costs NZ$20. Local bus access is also available in the city where an average one-way trip would cost NZ$1.80. It would be wise if you got a reloadable Metrocard as having one means gaining access to fare discounts and special promotions.

What to Do

ANTARCTIC CENTER
This facility is located near the airport. It is an excellent destination to consider if travelers are interested in Antarctica as it offers information on the local environment and wildlife in this particular continent.

There is a simulated environment that you can take part in. An actual Hägglund Antarctic vehicle is also available on-site for those who want to take it for a spin.

GONDOLA RIDE
In the southern suburban area is a place where you can experience riding in a gondola. Gondolas run through canals offering visitors extraordinary views of the city center and its surrounding areas.

LYTTELTON
The Lyttelton Farmers Market is an excellent place to source fresh and authentic local ingredients. Seasonal produce, freshly baked bread, honey, eggs, cheese, and relish are some of the most popular products here. There are times when local musicians serenade the shopping crowd with lively local tunes.

FESTIVALS
A number of festivals take place in Christchurch. Usually, events happen every month so it would be best to check a gig calendar when planning an itinerary. The most popular event here is the Festival of Romance. It is a local take on Valentine's Day and takes place over a span of ten days.

CANTERBURY MUSEUM
Admission to the museum is free. Here is where visitors can take a look at colonial displays, Maori artifacts, and visiting exhibitions.

MAORI IMMERSION
Experiencing the local Maori culture is a treat in itself. A trip to Kotane will satisfy the Maori warrior in each traveler. It is a cultural center located by the Willowbank reserve. Village tours, performance shows, and dinner are offered as a package to visitors. Each one costs NZ$165 and lasts for a whole day.

WILLOWBANK WILDLIFE RESERVE
This park houses native bird life. It is also known for offering a series of nocturnal kiwi tours. It is a great place to visit especially when traveling with children.

PORT HILLS
The Port Hills offer a series of trails that will satisfy the need of any outdoorsman. It offers one of the best views of the city not to mention the Banks Peninsula and Southern Alps. It is a locally frequented exercise spot as well.

CATHEDRAL SQUARE
Located at the city center, this is where all fairs, markets, and public hangouts can be found. It is an excellent location for those who want to mingle with the locals. Weekends here mean various events that you can attend.

BONE CARVING
Those who want to try their hands at bone carving should go to the local Bone Dude. It would be best to make an early reservation as only one session is offered per day Mondays through Fridays at noon until 4 in the afternoon. It is also

open on Saturdays where the session lasts from ten in the morning until 1 in the afternoon.

MONA VALE

This is an Elizabethan-style structure that sits on a large parcel of well-maintained land. It is known for the pre-made picnics. You can actually order a picnic set in advance and have a picnic within the compound.

HAGLEY PARK

Hagley Park offers wondrous botanic gardens making it a great alternative for those who want to take a relaxing stroll or tranquil jog away from the hustle and bustle of the city grounds.

SOMO

Somo stands for the South of Moorhouse. It is a hip area that serves as the hub for local artists and other creative individuals. It is also home to a series of unique restaurants, cafes, and pubs. Those who want to listen to live music will also find something satisfying at Somo.

Chapter 11: Queenstown

In New Zealand's South Island lies Queenstown, which is one of the most popular destinations in the country. Mountains and tiny walkable streets surround the phenomenal city. It is home to an amazing lake not to mention a mecca for adventure-related activities. The energy in this part of New Zealand is quite strong and this is why most visitors extend their trips especially those who are in the area for the first time.

Accommodations

Backpackers can easily find rooms here which cost around NZ$25-40 per night. Those who are interested in more private quarters can find ample space for NZ$70 a night. There are hotels which cost around NZ$80-120 per night as well.

Here are some of the best-rated accommodations in Queenstown:

THE SPIRE HOTEL QUEENSTOWN $532
This place is quite close to the Wakatipu and scenic reserve. This place is pretty upscale and comes with many great facilities. The views from the rooms are quite spectacular and will treat your senses. The food here is simply fantastic and will make you come back for more.

3-5 Church Lane

MATAKAURI LODGE
This is a 5 star hotel and provides you with some amazing views. It is also one of the best hotels to stay at in Queenstown. You will have access to some of the best amenities on offer in

Queenstown including 5 star suites containing flat screen televisions, minibars, refrigerators, and other world-class amenities. You are sure to have a splendid time when you stay at this hotel.

Glenorchy Road, P.O. Box 888

SOFITEL QUEENSTOWN HOTEL & SPA
Sofitel in Queenstown is a great place to consider for your stay. The quality is top notch and matches most other Sofitel hotels around the world. You can have access to deluxe rooms with amazing facilities. You can have a great time here and enjoy all the complimentary services such as the swimming pool, gymnasium and other such top class features.

8 Duke Street, P.O. Box 1797
00 64 3 450 0045

Other options
- THE DAIRY PRIVATE HOTEL
10 Isle Street
00 64 3 667 1584

- GLEBE APARTMENTS
2 Beetham Street
00 64 3 668 1210

- EICHARDT'S PRIVATE HOTEL
Marine Parade, P.O. Box 1340

- AZUR
23 MacKinnon Terrace, Sunshine Bay
00 64 3 668 4228

- VILLA DEL LAGO
249 Frankton Road
00 64 3 667 1587

- QUEENSTOWN PARK BOUTIQUE HOTEL
21 Robins Road
00 64 3 668 1244

- BROWNS BOUTIQUE HOTEL
26 Isle Street

Food and Beverage

A plate at one of the standard city restaurants can set you back about NZ$23. Those who plan on cooking their own food can set a weekly budget of around NZ$60-90. Fast food establishments are also accessible with meals costing anywhere from NZ$8-12 per meal.

Queenstown is a great place for you to try out authentic New Zealand cuisine. There are many restaurants to pick from and some of them are as under.

Restaurants in Queenstown

The Ballarat trading company

The Ballarat trading company is one of the best restaurants to visit in Queenstown. The place has been described as being quite old school in terms of the menu and the décor. You are sure to find an interesting meal here that you can savor with friends and family. The pub here is also famous and serves some amazing brews. This is a must visit in restaurant in Queenstown.

7-9 The Mall Queenstown 9300, +64 3 442 4222

Coyote grill

Established as recently as 2012, the coyote grill serves some authentic Mexican food. So if you are in the mood to savor some Mexican cuisine then it is best to head down to this specific restaurant. The place makes use of some authentic Mexican ingredients that are sure to please your palate. You can wash it all down with some tequila. The place is quite cool and offers an amazing ambience to its customers.

1/66 Shotover Street Queenstown 9300, +64 3 441 8562

Roaring Meg's restaurant

For all those looking for authentic New Zealand dishes such as the lamb grill can turn to the roaring Megs restaurant. The place serves up some amazing dishes that can be savored with some wine. The restaurant is quite old-fashioned in terms of the decor and makes for a comfortable place to enjoy a meal with family. The place has won many awards for the great food that it serves.

53 Shotover St Queenstown, +64 3 442 9676

Nightclubs/bars in Queenstown

Gibbstown Tavern

The Gibbston tavern is nothing short of a legendary place. Located in the famous Gibbston valley, this place is a must visit bar in Queenstown. Operated by some of the most experienced brewers, this place is a class apart. Not only can you savor the brew here but also enjoy your stay in this fancy place. You are sure to have an unforgettable time here as you tuck into some of the best food on offer in Queenstown.

Rapid 8 Coal Pit Road RD1 Queenstown 9371, +64 3 409 0508

Pub on Wharf

If you want to party the night away then Pub on Wharf is the place to be. Pub on Wharf is a happening place in Queenstown that offers some amazing craft beer in pints. The prices here are quite reasonable and will ensure that you have a hearty meal. You can also savor the amazing food on offer here and have a memorable night out with friends.

88 Beach Street Queenstown 9300, +64 3 441 2155

Morrison's Irish pub

If you are craving for some tap beer then Morrison's Irish pub is a must visit. The place is always filled with people looking to have a great time. The food here is delicious and sure to leave you craving for more. Morrison's Irish pub is a very hospitable place offering some amazing drinks. You can enjoy some live music 3 nights here and make the most of the pub's lively atmosphere.

Level 1 Stratton House 16-24 Beach Street Queenstown +64 3 441 3095

Transportation

The city is rather small and this is an advantage for travelers as there are plenty of pedestrian-friendly roads. This means that you can save a lot of money by walking to and from different locations. If necessary, there is a local bus service with rides available throughout the day.

What to Do

LAKE SAILING
Queenstown is known for having one of the most beautiful lakes in New Zealand. It surrounds the island and offers opportunities for activities such as boating, sailing, and swimming.

FERGBURGER
There is a local restaurant that every visitor must try out when they arrive in Queenstown, as it will be regretful to miss the best burger joint in the country. Aside from their deliciously humungous burgers, the local fries that complement the meal are also to die for.

Because of its popularity, Fergburger always has a long queue throughout the day so be ready to fall in line and be as patient as possible. The great thing about this place is that they have a burger option for vegans as well.

LOCAL MARKETS/ROADSIDE STANDS
Especially during the summer season, local farmers markets offer some of the best fruits and vegetables that money can buy.

BUS TOUR
For those who are traveling to the city for the first time, a guided bus tour is an excellent way to see the sights. It typically costs around NZ$70 per person and depending on the season may require advanced reservations.

SHOTOVER
The Shotover is a water jet. It is a speedboat that runs extremely fast. Trips are usually taken around local rivers. It is

an excellent activity for adrenalin junkies to try out. Usually driven on shallow waters, some might think that it could crash at any moment but it does not. This is actually where most of the rush comes from.

NEVIS
The Nevis jump is a well-known activity in these parts. It involves bungee jumping off of a 500-foot platform - one of the highest the world has ever seen!

ZIPLINE
Zip lining is fairly new but increasingly popular in Queenstown. It starts from the mountain area down a forestry trail. Throughout the line, you will see breathtaking views of the city and local lake.

HELICOPTER TOURS
Queenstown also offers helicopter tours above the grandiose mountainside - The Remarkables. Aside from this, you also get a bird's eye view of a lush rainforest and secluded alpine rivers.

SKIING/SNOWBOARDING
Skiing is a very popular activity in this part of the country during the winter months, snowboarding as well mind you, as the mountainous terrain provides for some of the best ski slopes available. There are different trails for novices, experienced riders, and experts.

VINEYARD EXPLORATION
New Zealand is known for its excellent wine and some of the best and largest vineyards can be found in Queenstown. Do try the various wine tasting trips and vineyard tours that are

available from several tour operators. The main type of wine produced in this area is white wine.

UNDERWATER OBSERVATORY

There is an underwater observatory lined with massive windows providing an interactive exhibit of the local lake. You can come here and see the schools of large fish that inhabit these waters. There are fish feeders installed around the facility as well. It only costs NZ$1 which is pretty affordable for an excellent experience.

ST, PETER'S CHURCH

The church was built in 1863 and is considered to be one of New Zealand's historical treasures. It started with a wooden structure that was then upgraded to have stone foundations for better support. Marvel at the beautiful detailing around the church and see the famous lectern carved in the shape of an eagle.

OFF-ROADING ADVENTURE

Off-roading is another excellent activity to try out when in Queenstown. Different operators can be found in the city offering 4WD rides to those who want to view the canyons and rivers. Expect to get splashed in one way or another. The average cost for this runs at about NZ$100-200 per person for a half-day arrangement.

BIRDLIFE PARK

The Kiwi Birdlife Park is home to over ten thousand species of flora, fauna, and birds especially Kiwis. These are flightless birds native to New Zealand. You can take a walk around the park and take part in a cultural show put on by the local Maoris.

HORSEBACK RIDING

Since Queenstown is home to mountainous terrain, it offers the perfect setting for horseback riding. Different tours are available here from half-day to multi-day options. Aside from the mountainside, horseback tours will lead you around the areas of the local rivers and lake.

Chapter 12: Waitomo

An interesting story about Waitomo is that it actually rose from the ocean floor. It has been over thirty million years since then but the area still possesses something unique - an underground limestone formation - the only one of its kind in New Zealand.

Aside from seeing the amazing underground caves, a number of travelers find themselves in Waitomo for its natural wonders as well as the famous glowworms. A bit of information about these glowworms is that they are not actual worms. They are organisms that float through the rivers in these underground caves. A trip to Waitomo can prove to be not only entertaining but also educational.

Accommodations

A dorm bed will cost you about NZ$25-35 while private rooms will cost around NZ$75. For hotels, the rooms start at about NZ$90 a night.

Here are some of the best-rated accommodations in Waitomo:

JUNO HALL BACKPACKERS
Set 2 km away from the Waitomo caves, this place is set on a farm. There are both dormitories and rooms available here that you can use as per your convenience. The rooms are all reasonably priced and will help you enjoy a great stay. You can enjoy common amenities such as the tennis court. This is a pet friendly hotel that is sure to help you and your pets have a great time.

600 Waitomo Caves Road
00 64 7 878 7649

CAMP KIWI HOLIDAY PARK

The holiday park is a great place for you to relax and rewind. You can enjoy the natural settings and have a good time exploring the nature. You will have access to basic rooms and amenities such as televisions, minibars, refrigerators etc. The camp is one of the best in this locality and a great place to stay at.

7 Domain Drive, Otorohanga
00 64 7 873 7391

KIWI PAKA WAITOMO

The kiwi paka Waitomo is a great place to stay at. It has top class facilities on offer and will ensure that you have a great time. You can enjoy a family holiday here, as the suites are equipped with all the basic amenities including televisions, refrigerator, kitchenette etc.

Hotel Access Road, Waitomo Caves
00 64 7 878 3395

Other options
- OTOROHANGA HOLIDAY PARK
12 Huiputea Drive, Otorohanga
00 64 7 873 7253

- KAMAHI COTTAGE
229 Barber Road, Otorohanga
00 64 7 873 0849

- RANGIMARIE BUSH RETREAT
2350 Kawhia Road, Te Awamutu
00 64 7 871 9533

- ABSEIL INN BED AND BREAKFAST
709 Waitomo Caves Road
00 64 7 878 7815
- WAITOMO TOP 10 HOLIDAY PARK
Waitomo Caves Road
00 64 7 878 7639

- WAITOMO LODGE HOTEL
64 Te Kumi Road, Te Kuiti
00 64 7 878 0003

- REDWOOD LODGE
222 Puketawai Road, Otorohanga
00 64 7 873 6685

Food and Beverage

Compared to other places in the country, Waitomo is more on the rural end so there aren't plenty of high-end restaurants in town. This is actually great because it means that the food here is rather inexpensive. Fine fare is available at the local pubs and a meal will roughly cost about NZ$15 to start. Choosing to do the cooking at home means a week's budget of around NZ$50 for groceries.

Waitomo has a handful of good restaurants that you can visit during your stay.

Restaurants in Waitomo

Huhu
Huhu is a great little restaurant to visit in Waitomo. The place offers some amazing food and drinks. The brews here are quite amazing and will make you want more. The food is incredible with the slow cooked lamb, and organic rib eye steak making

for a must try. You must also savor the teriyaki salmon here, which makes for one of their signature dishes.

10 Waitomo Caves Rd, 07-878 6674

Morepork café
A good place to have a nice meal is the Morepork café. The place is a small little joint that serves some great pizza. You can savor the breakfast, lunch and dinner here and have a great time with friends and family.

Kiwi Paka, Hotel Access Rd, 07-878 3395

Roselands
Roselands is a great little place to visit in Waitomo. You will have the chance to savor amazing food such as beef stew and amazing barbeques. It is a nice place for you to grab some comfort food and relish the same.

Transportation
There are buses in Waitomo that can bring you to the famous caves. There are tour shuttles as well.

What to Do
The activities available in this part of the country are more nature-related and here are some of them.

BLACK WATER RAFTING
Everyone is quite familiar with the concept of white water rafting. What makes black water rafting different is that it involves traversing rough waters in a tube and the rafting takes place inside the cave system. These tubing experiences take place inside the Ruakuri Cave and there are different tour packages to choose from.

CANOEING

A gentler activity available in this part of the country is canoeing. You can rent canoes for a minimal fee and explore the surrounding rivers via slow and relaxed unrushed paddling. The playful water will definitely calm your nerves.

RUAKURI CAVE

It was the Maori people who discovered the Ruakuri Cave about five centuries ago and it was named after a local wild dog specie that used to live by the entrance of the cave. For the Maori, this cave exists as a burial ground or Wahi Tapu.

CAVE MUSEUM

There is something known as the Museum of Caves in this part of the country and those who are interested in learning about these natural structures, glowworms included, can visit the facility for some local knowledge. There are exhibits about the local ecosystem, cave formation processes, and how glowworms live. Admission is free.

WAITOMO GLOWWORM TOUR

In this part of the country, it is easy to take a guided walk through the glowworm caves. There are smaller caves that take a shorter amount of time to traverse and these come with cheaper price tags as well. A typical tour lasts for about an hour.

The glowworms can be seen floating across the underground rivers some of which hang above the caves. Those who have a bit more time to spare can engage in a rafting trip that lasts about three to five hours.

OTOROHANGA KIWI HOUSE AND NATIVE BIRD PARK
Waitomo is also known for Otorohanga, which is a sanctuary for the Kiwi, other bird species, and other kinds of local wildlife.

ANIMAL SHEARING
Yes, the shearing of animals is an attraction in Waitomo and it can be experienced at The Shearing Shed that is home to plenty of Angora rabbits. The fur shaved from these animals is used to make a variety of wool products. You can also find shop selling wool products nearby.

ARANUI CAVE
In Waitomo, the Aranui Cave is one of the smaller caves that are accessible to travelers. It is small but has quite a large deposit of natural limestone, which makes it unique. It is a beautiful natural marvel.

ALTURE GARDEN TREKKING
The Altura Gardens is an excellent place for trekking. It also doubles as a wildlife park. It spans five acres and is home to various types of animals including about eighty-five bird species. They offer horseback services as trekking by foot could take an extremely long time to finish. Riding a horse ensures that you are able to cover more ground in less time. For those who like a little more of adventure, you can find great companions to walk the trek with you by foot.

KIWI CULTURE SHOW
Cultural shows are quite popular in countries such as New Zealand and there is a countryside theater in Waitomo that offers hour-long presentations on a regular basis. The skit encompasses everything from the local culture to the local humor. In this particular show, audience participation is taken

seriously so expect to join in on the action. You will not only be entertained but will also learn a lot of new things regarding the culture of New Zealand.

Conclusion

Once again thank you for choosing *Lost Travelers*!

New Zealand is the land of what dreams are made of. Thanks to its ample natural as well as manmade beauty and it clean and fresh environment, New Zealand is quickly becoming one of the hottest tourist destinations of the world. It is also becoming highly popular as a honeymoon destination, thanks to its soothingly romantic and pleasant ambience. So, pick New Zealand if you want the best of both worlds! I hope this book was able to provide you with the best travel tips when visiting New Zealand.

And we hope you enjoy your travels.

"Travel Brings Power And Love Back To Your Life"

- Rumi

Finally, if you enjoyed this book, then I'd like to ask you for a favor, would you be kind enough to leave a review for this book on Amazon? It'd be greatly appreciated!

- Simply search the keywords "New Zealand Travel Guide" on Amazon or go to our Author page "Lost Travelers" to review.

Please know that your satisfaction is important to us. If you were not happy with the book, please email us with the reason so we may serve you more accordingly next time.

- Email: info@losttravelers.com

Thank you and good luck!

NOTES

NOTES

NOTES

NOTES

Preview Of 'London: The Ultimate London Travel Guide By A Traveler For A Traveler

London, Great Britain's glamorous capital, stands as one of the world's major hubs of finance, arts, fashion and overall entertainment. The city's history is traceable back to the Roman times, with such notable figures of history such as William the Conqueror having their lives shaped in one way or the other by the city. The truth is that, whether you realize it or not, London has shaped your destiny in one-way or the other. London, being the huge city that it is, is inexhaustible- you could spend months touring it and still get to barely know it. There is perhaps no city in the world that has such a wide variety of people, all living in such deep-seated harmony.

This diversity is what makes London something of an uncut diamond- if you approach it from a differing angle each time, it will present itself in a completely fresh color and shape. From the famous stories associated with it to the distinct high style, London manages to be multiple things in every passing moment... TO BE CONTINUED!

Check out the rest of London: The Ultimate London Travel Guide on Amazon by simply searching it.

Check Out Our Other Books

Below you'll find some of our other popular books that are on Amazon and Kindle as well. Simply search the titles below to check them out. Alternatively, you can visit our author page (Lost Travelers) on Amazon to see other work done by us.

- Vienna: The Ultimate Vienna Travel Guide By A Traveler For A Traveler

- Barcelona: The Ultimate Barcelona Travel Guide By A Traveler For A Traveler

- London: The Ultimate London Travel Guide By A Traveler For A Traveler

- Istanbul: The Ultimate Istanbul Travel Guide By A Traveler For A Traveler

- Vietnam: The Ultimate Vietnam Travel Guide By A Traveler For A Traveler

- Peru: The Ultimate Peru Travel Guide By A Traveler For A Traveler

- Australia: The Ultimate Australia Guide By A Traveler For A Traveler

- Japan: The Ultimate Japan Travel Guide By A Traveler For A Traveler

- [Thailand: The Ultimate Thailand Travel Guide By A Traveler For A Traveler](#)

- [Dublin: The Ultimate Dublin Travel Guide By A Traveler For A Traveler](#)

- [Tokyo: The Ultimate Tokyo Travel Guide By A Traveler For A Traveler](#)

- [Iceland: The Ultimate Iceland Travel Guide By A Traveler For A Traveler](#)

- [Santorini: The Ultimate Santorini Travel Guide By A Traveler For A Traveler](#)

- [Italy: The Ultimate Italy Travel Guide By A Traveler For A Traveler](#)

You can simply search for these titles on the Amazon website to find them.